FUN FASHIONS™

Contemporary Outfits to Knit fo

Designs by Andra Knight-Bowman

HOUSE of
WHITE
BIRCHES

PUBLISHERS
SINCE 1947

Table of Contents

Introduction

Dolls love fashion just as much as the people who love dressing them up. Whether you are a knitter, a doll collector or a girl who loves to dress up her dolls, you will enjoy getting your hands on these new outfits for the ever-popular 18-inch dolls.

We have included something for every season. Head back to school with Preppy Patty, to a water front vacation with Beachwear Billie or perhaps head out in the snow with Wintertime Winnie. Each outfit comes with the accessories you need to complete the look.

We hope you will enjoy making these fun new outfits for your 18-inch dolls just as much as the dolls will love wearing them!

Meet the Designer

At the age of 7, I learned to knit, and I was a natural at the craft. I soon started making sweaters for my Barbie dolls and my dog, Mitzi. Designing entered my life at an early age.

In high school, I had the opportunity to work at a local yarn shop. It was there I learned about fibers and sweater designing. My goal in life was to own a yarn shop of my own.

PHOTO BY GREG SEAVER

I opened Knits & Pearls in 2004 and introduced many of my designs from previous years to my customers. Since then I have created many more designs. They have been published in numerous magazines and books, including *Easy Cable Knits for All Seasons*, *Modular Knitting Made Easy, Fun to Knit Doll Clothes* and *Seamless (or Nearly Seamless) Knits*. I feel so blessed and am grateful for everyone who has believed in me.

I reside in Johnson City, Tenn., with my wonderful husband, Terry, who has been a gem through book writings and two furry kids (cats), Billie and Blue. I just couldn't ask for a better life!

Preppy Patty

Size
Fits 18-inch doll

Finished Measurements
Chest: 13½ inches
Cardigan length: 6½ inches
Skirt length: 7 inches

Materials
- Patons Classic Wool (light worsted weight; 100% wool; 210 yds/100g per ball): 1 ball each bright red #00230 (A) and dark gray mix #00225 (B); approx 5 yds winter white #00201 (C)
- Size 6 (4mm) needles
- Size 7 (4.5mm) needles, and 1 extra needle for 3-needle bind-off, or size needed to obtain gauge
- Stitch holders
- Removable stitch markers
- 3 (⅝-inch) buttons
- 12 inches ⅛-inch-wide elastic, slightly stretched

Gauge
20 sts and 28 rows = 4 inches/10cm in St st with larger needles.

To save time, take time to check gauge.

Special Technique
3-Needle Bind-Off: With RS tog and needles parallel, using a 3rd needle, knit tog a st from front needle with 1 from the back. *Knit tog a st from front and back needles, and slip first st over 2nd to bind off. Rep from * across, and then fasten off last st.

Pattern Note
When working color pattern on fronts, use intarsia technique, using separate lengths of yarn for each colored section; bring new color up from under old color to lock them.

Cardigan

Back
With smaller needles and A, cast on 34 sts.

Knit 3 rows.

Change to larger needles and work in St st for 40 rows.

Place sts on a holder.

Left Front

With smaller needles and A, cast on 16 sts.

Knit 3 rows.

Change to larger needles and work 24 rows in St st following Left Front chart.

Neck shaping
Dec row (RS): Knit to last 3 sts, k2tog, k1—15 sts.

Continue in St st following chart and rep Dec row [every RS row] 6 more times—9 sts.

Work even through Row 40.

Place sts on holder.

Right Front

Work as for left front through Row 24, following Right Front chart.

Neck shaping
Dec row (RS): K1, ssk, knit to end—15 sts.

Continue in St st and rep Dec row [every RS row] 6 more times—9 sts.

Work even through Row 40.

Place sts on holder.

Sleeves

With smaller needles and A, cast on 21 sts.

Knit 3 rows.

Change to larger needles and work in St st for 4 rows.

Inc row (RS): K1, M1, knit to last st, M1, k1—23 sts.

Rep Inc row [every 4th row] 3 more times—29 sts.

Work even until sleeve measures 3½ inches.

Bind off loosely.

Finishing
Weave in ends. Block pieces to finished measurements.

Transfer front sts to needle; transfer first and last 9 back sts to another needle, leaving center 16 sts on holder for back neck.

Join shoulders using 3-Needle Bind-Off.

Place marker 3 inches from shoulders on each side of shoulder.

Sew in sleeves between markers.

Sew side and sleeve seams.

Band
Pick-up row (RS): Using smaller needles, pick up and knit 34 sts along right front; k16 across back neck, pick up and knit 34 sts along left front—84 sts.

Row 1 (WS): Knit.

Row 2 (buttonhole row): K1, [yo, k2tog, k6] 3 times, knit to end.

Row 3: Knit.

Bind off loosely.

Sew buttons to left front opposite buttonholes.

Skirt

Front/Back
Make 2

With smaller needles and B, cast on 35 sts.

Knit 3 rows.

Change to larger needles and work in St st until piece measures 6 inches, ending with a WS row.

Dec row (RS): K2, k2tog, [k5, k2tog] 4 times, end k3—30 sts.

Work 5 more rows in St st.

Turning ridge (RS): Purl.

Beg with a purl row, work 5 rows in St st.

Finishing
Weave in ends. Block pieces to measurements given on schematic.

Sew side seams.

Sew piece of elastic tog to form a ring.

Fold waistband along turning ridge and sew the band in place over the elastic.

Bag

With larger needles and A, cast on 21 sts.

Work in St st and alternate A and B [every 2 rows] 11 times.

Bind off loosely.

Fold piece in half widthwise and sew 1 side seam.

With RS facing and B, pick up and knit 35 sts along the top edge.

Knit 3 rows.

Bind off loosely.

Sew the other side seam.

Strap

With larger needles and B, cast on 3 sts.

Work in garter st for 13 inches, slightly stretched.

Bind off loosely.

Sew straps to inside of the bag at the side seams. ●

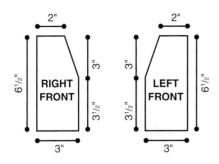

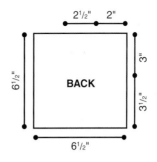

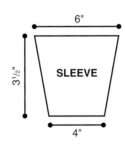

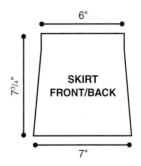

STITCH & COLOR KEY
- ◼ With A, k on RS, p on WS
- ◪ With A, k2tog
- ◪ With A, ssk
- ◼ With B, k on RS, p on WS
- ☐ With C, k on RS, p on WS

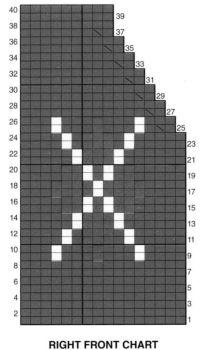

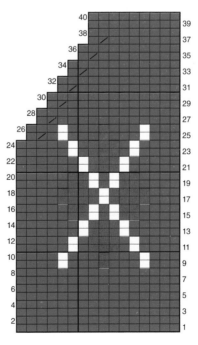

RIGHT FRONT CHART   **LEFT FRONT CHART**

Wintertime Winnie

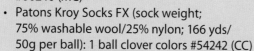

Skill Level
■■■□ INTERMEDIATE

Size
Fits 18-inch doll

Finished Measurements
Chest: 13 inches
Length: 11 inches

Materials
- Patons Classic Wool (light worsted weight; 100% wool; 210 yds/ 100g per ball): 1 ball leaf green #00240 (MC)
- Patons Kroy Socks FX (sock weight; 75% washable wool/25% nylon; 166 yds/ 50g per ball): 1 ball clover colors #54242 (CC)
- Size 4 (3.5mm) needles
- Size 7 (4.5mm) needles, and 1 extra needle for 3-needle bind-off, or size needed to obtain gauge
- Size H/8 (5mm) crochet hook
- Removable stitch markers
- Stitch holders
- 3 (½-inch) buttons

Gauge
19 sts and 38 rows = 4 inches/10cm in garter st with larger needles and MC.

To save time, take time to check gauge.

Special Techniques
Crochet Cast-On: Place a slip knot of working yarn on crochet hook. Hold crochet hook in your right hand and a knitting needle in your left hand. *Make a yo around needle, going from back to front; catch yarn with crochet hook and pull it through loop on hook to ch-1; rep from * until you have 1 fewer st than required for your cast-on. Slip loop on crochet hook to needle for last st.

3-Needle Bind-Off: With RS tog and needles parallel, using a 3rd needle, knit tog a st from front needle with 1 from the back. *Knit tog a st from front and back needles, and slip first st over 2nd to bind off. Rep from * across, and then fasten off last st.

Make 1 (M1): Insert LH needle from front to back under horizontal strand between last st worked and next st on RH needle; knit into back of resulting loop.

Pattern Notes
The coat is worked in garter stitch, beginning with the bottom half, which is worked from side to side. The fronts and back are picked up along the edge of the bottom half and worked to the neck. After the shoulders are joined, the sleeves are picked up along the armholes and worked down to the cuff.

On the coat, slip the first stitch of every row purlwise throughout.

Coat

Bottom Half
Using Crochet Cast-On method, larger needle and MC, cast on 31 sts.

Rows 1–124: Mark first row as RS; slipping first st of every row, knit all rows—62 ridges.

Place markers at end of 17th and 47th ridges for placement of back and fronts.

Buttonhole row (RS): Knit to last 5 sts, yo, k2tog, k3.

Knit 3 rows.

Bind off loosely. Do not cut yarn.

Right Front
Pick-up row (RS): Using larger needle and MC, pick up and knit 17 sts to first marker; turn.

Rows 1–7: Sl 1, knit to end.

Buttonhole row (RS): Sl 1, k2, yo, k2tog, knit to end.

Knit 11 rows, then work Buttonhole row again.

Work even until front measures 4½ inches from Pick-up row, ending with a WS row.

Place sts on a holder.

Back

Pick-up row (RS): Using larger needle and MC, pick up and knit 30 sts between first and 2nd markers.

Slipping first st of every row, work even in garter st until back measures 4½ inches from Pick-up row, ending with a WS row.

Place sts on a holder.

Left Front

Pick-up row (RS): Using larger needle and MC, pick up and knit 17 sts from 2nd marker to end.

Slipping first st of every row, work even in garter st until front measures 4½ inches from Pick-up row, ending with a WS row.

Place sts on a holder.

Join first and last 9 back sts to corresponding front sts using 3-Needle Bind-Off for shoulder, leaving center 12 back sts and rem 8 sts each front on holders for collar.

Sleeves

Place markers 3 inches down from each shoulder.

Pick-up row (RS): Using larger needle and MC, pick up and knit 1 st in each ridge between markers.

Slipping first st of every row, work even in garter st until sleeve measures 4 inches, ending with a RS row.

Bind off loosely.

Rep for other sleeve.

Collar

Transfer front and back collar sts to larger needle in following order: left front, back, right front.

With RS facing and using larger needle, k8 right front sts, pick up and knit 3 sts at shoulder seam, k12 back sts, pick up 3 sts at shoulder seam, k8 left front sts—34 sts.

Slipping first st of every row, work in garter st for 1½ inches, ending with a RS row.

Bind off loosely.

Finishing

Weave in ends. Block coat to finished measurements.

Sew sleeve and side seams. Sew buttons opposite buttonholes.

Scarf

With smaller needles and CC, cast on 18 sts.

Work in St st for 20 inches.

Bind off loosely.

Sew side seams to form a tube.

Fringe

Cut 32 (4-inch) strands of CC.

Use 4 strands tog for each fringe. *Fold 1 set of 4 strands in half. Beg at corner of 1 short end, use crochet hook to draw folded end from front to back. Pull loose ends through folded section. Draw knot up firmly. Rep from *, placing 4 evenly spaced fringes along each short end. Trim ends even.

Beret

With smaller needles and CC, cast on 70 sts.

Work 5 rows in k1, p1 rib and inc 1 st on last row—71 sts.

Beg with a RS row, work 6 rows in St st.

Inc row (RS): [K7, M1] 10 times, k1—81 sts.

Continuing in St st, work 5 rows even.

Inc row (RS): [K8, M1] 10 times, k1—91 sts.

Continuing in St st, work 5 rows even.

Shape crown
Row 1 (RS): [K8, k2tog, place marker] 9 times, k1—82 sts.

Row 2 and all WS rows: Purl.

Dec row: [Knit to 2 sts before marker, k2tog] 9 times, k1—73 sts.

Rep Dec row [every RS row] 6 more times—19 sts.

Next RS row: [K2tog] 9 times, k1—10 sts.

Next RS row: [K2tog] 5 times—5 sts.

Cut yarn, leaving a 12-inch tail. Using tapestry needle, thread tail through rem sts and pull tight.

Sew seam from top to cast-on edge.

Weave in ends.

Mittens
Make 2

With smaller needles and CC, cast on 22 sts.

Work 5 rows in k1, p1 rib.

Beg with a RS row, work 4 rows in St st.

Gusset
Row 1 (RS): K10, M1, k2, M1, k10—24 sts.

Row 2 and all WS rows: Purl.

Row 3: K10, M1, k4, M1, k10—26 sts.

Row 5: K10, M1, k6, M1, k10—28 sts.

Row 7: K10; place next 8 sts on holder for thumb, k10—20 sts.

Continue in St st and work 7 rows.

Next 2 RS rows: K2tog across—5 sts.

Cut yarn, leaving a 6-inch tail. Using tapestry needle, thread tail through rem sts, and pull tight.

Sew seam from top to cast-on edge.

Thumb
Transfer 8 thumb sts to smaller needle.

Beg with a RS row, work 4 rows in St st.

Next row: K2tog across—4 sts.

Cut yarn, leaving a 6-inch tail. Using tapestry needle, thread tail through rem sts and pull tight.

Sew thumb seam.

Weave in all ends. ●

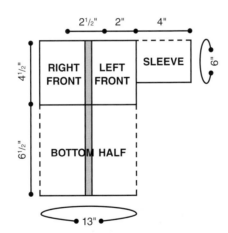

Sassy Sally

Size
Fits 18-inch doll

Finished Measurements
Chest: 11 inches
Length: 11 inches

Materials
- NaturallyCaron.com Country (worsted weight; 75% microdenier acrylic/ 25% merino wool; 185 yds/ 85g per ball): 2 balls deep purple #0014
- Size 7 (4.5mm) needles
- Size 8 (5mm) needles or size needed to obtain gauge

4 MEDIUM

Gauge
18 sts and 24 rows = 4 inches/10cm in St st with larger needles.

To save time, take time to check gauge.

Special Abbreviation
Make 1 (M1): Insert LH needle from front to back under running thread between last st worked and next st on RH needle; knit into back of resulting loop.

Dress

Back
With smaller needles, cast on 100 sts.

Row 1 (RS): Knit.

Change to larger needles and continue in St st for 7 rows.

Dec row (RS): K2tog across—50 sts.

Next row (WS): Knit.

Work in St st until piece measures 6 inches, ending with a WS row.

Waistband
Rep Dec row—25 sts.

Knit 7 rows.

Back neck
Row 1 (RS): K12, join a new ball of yarn, bind off center st, k12.

Row 2: Using separate balls of yarn, purl across each side.

Row 3: Knit to 3 sts before center st, k2tog, k1; k1, ssk, knit to end—11 sts each side.

Row 4: Purl.

Rep last 2 rows twice more—9 sts each side.

Work even in St st until piece measures 2 inches from beg of waistband, ending with a WS row.

Armholes
Bind off 3 sts at beg of next 2 rows—6 sts each side.

Work even until armholes measure 3 inches, ending with a WS row.

Bind off loosely.

Front
Work same as for back through waistband.

Work in St st until piece measures 2 inches from beg of waistband, ending with a WS row.

Armholes
Bind off 3 sts at beg of next 2 rows—19 sts.

Work even until armhole measures 1½ inches, ending with a WS row.

Front neck
Row 1 (RS): K8, join a new ball of yarn, bind off center 3 sts, k8.

Rows 2 and 3: Working both sides at once, dec 1 st at each neck edge—6 sts each side.

Work even until armholes measure 3 inches, ending with a WS row.

Bind off.

Sleeves

With smaller needles, cast on 18 sts.

Row 1 (WS): Knit 1 row.

Rows 2 (RS) and 3: Change to larger needles; work in St st.

Row 4 (inc): K1, *M1, k1; rep from * to end—35 sts.

Work 3 rows even.

Shape cap

Bind off 3 sts at beg of next 2 rows—29 sts.

Dec row (RS): K1, ssk, knit to last 3 sts, k2tog, k1—27 sts.

Purl 1 row.

Rep Dec row—25 sts.

Work even until cap measures 2 inches, ending with a WS row.

Next row (RS): K1, [k2tog] 12 times—13 sts.

Next row: P1, [p2tog] 6 times—7 sts.

Bind off loosely.

Finishing

Weave in ends and block pieces.

Neckband

Sew left shoulder seam.

With RS facing and smaller needles, starting at right shoulder, pick up and knit approx 55 sts around front and back neck.

Knit 1 row.

Bind off loosely.

Sew right shoulder seam. Set in sleeves. Sew side and sleeve seams.

Back Sash

With larger needles, cast on 56 sts.

Knit 1 row.

Dec row: K1, ssk, knit to last 3 sts, k2tog, k1—54 sts.

Rep Dec row [every other row] twice more—50 sts.

Knit 1 row.

Bind off loosely.

Flower

With larger needles, cast on 8 sts.

Row 1 (RS): Knit.

Rows 2, 4 and 6 (WS): Purl.

Row 3: Inc in each st across—16 sts.

Row 5: Inc in each st across—32 sts.

Bind off loosely.

Roll flower into a spiral with the purl side to the outside and tack at base.

Sew flower to center of sash, and then sew center of sash to center of waistband. ●

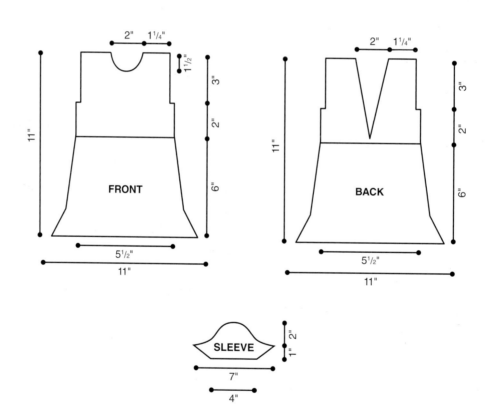

Holiday Holly

Size
Fits 18-inch doll

Finished Measurements
Capris length: 7½ inches
Moebius chest: 16 inches

Materials
- Lion Brand Yarn Vanna's Glamour (sport weight; 96% acrylic/ 4% metallic polyester; 202 yds/ 50g per ball): 1 ball each jewel #146 (MC) and onyx #153 (CC)
- Size 5 (3.75mm) needles or size needed to obtain gauge
- Cable needle
- Removable stitch markers
- Snap closure
- 12 inches ⅛-inch-wide elastic

Gauge
24 sts and 30 rows = 4 inches/10cm in St st.

To save time, take time to check gauge.

Special Abbreviations
2 over 2 Right Ribbed Cross (2/2 RRC): Sl 2 to cn and hold in back; k1, p1; k1, p1 from cn.

Make 1 (M1): Insert LH needle from front to back under horizontal strand between last st worked and next st on RH needle; knit into back of resulting loop.

Pattern Note
Capris are worked in 2 pieces from the waist down.

Capris

Left Side
With CC, cast on 36 sts.

Work 5 rows in St st.

Hem turning row (WS): Knit 1 row for turning edge.

Work even in St st until piece measures 1½ inches from beg, ending with a WS row.

Inc row (RS): Knit to last st, M1, k1—37 sts.

Rep Inc row [every 4 rows] 5 more times—42 sts.

Work even until piece measures 4½ inches, ending with a WS row; place a marker at each side.

Work even until piece measures 5 inches, ending with a WS row.

Dec row (RS): Knit to last 3 sts, k2tog, k1—41 sts.

Rep Dec row [every 4 rows] 5 more times—36 sts.

Work even until piece measures 8 inches, ending with a RS row.

Knit 3 rows.

Bind off loosely.

Right Side
Work as for Left Side until piece measures 1½ inches, ending with a WS row.

Inc row (RS): K1, M1, knit to end—37 sts.

Rep Inc row [every 4 rows] 5 more times—42 sts.

Work even until piece measures 4½ inches, ending with a WS row; place a marker at each side.

Work even until piece measures 5 inches, ending with a WS row.

Dec row (RS): K1, ssk, knit to end—41 sts.

Rep Dec row [every 4 rows] 5 more times—36 sts.

Work even until piece measures 8 inches, ending with a RS row.

Knit 3 rows.

Bind off loosely.

Finishing
Weave in all ends. Block pieces to schematic measurements.

Sew back seam (inc edge) from waist to marker. Sew front seam (straight edge) from waist to marker. Sew leg seams.

Overlap ends of elastic and sew tog to make an 11-inch circle. Fold waist hem down along turning ridge covering elastic; sew hem in place.

Moebius

With MC, cast on 25 sts.

Rows 1–6: Sl 1, [k5, (k1, p1) twice] twice, k6.

Row 7: Sl 1, [k5, 2/2 RRC] twice, k6.

Rows 8–12: Rep Row 1.

Rep Rows 1–12 until piece measures 16 inches, ending with a WS row.

Bind off loosely.

Finishing

Give piece ½ twist. Sew the cast-on edge to the bound-off edge.

Purse

With CC, cast on 15 sts.

Work in St st for 13 rows.

Next row (WS): Knit across for bottom turning edge.

Work 13 rows in St st, ending with a RS row.

Flap

Knit 3 rows.

Dec row (RS): K1, ssk, knit to last 3 sts, k2tog, k1—13 sts.

Knit 1 row.

Rep [last 2 rows] 4 times—5 sts.

Next row (RS): K1, k3tog, k1—3 sts.

Last row (WS): K3tog—1 st.

Fasten off.

Strap

Cast on 78 sts.

Knit 3 rows.

Bind off loosely.

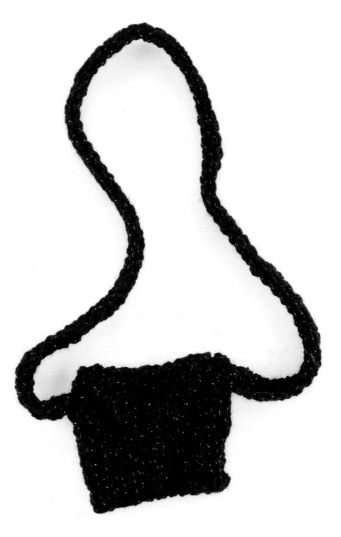

Finishing

Fold purse along bottom turning edge so that cast-on edge is even with beg of flap. Sew side seams.

Sew ends of strap to inside of purse at side seams.

Sew snap closure to outside of purse and WS of flap. ●

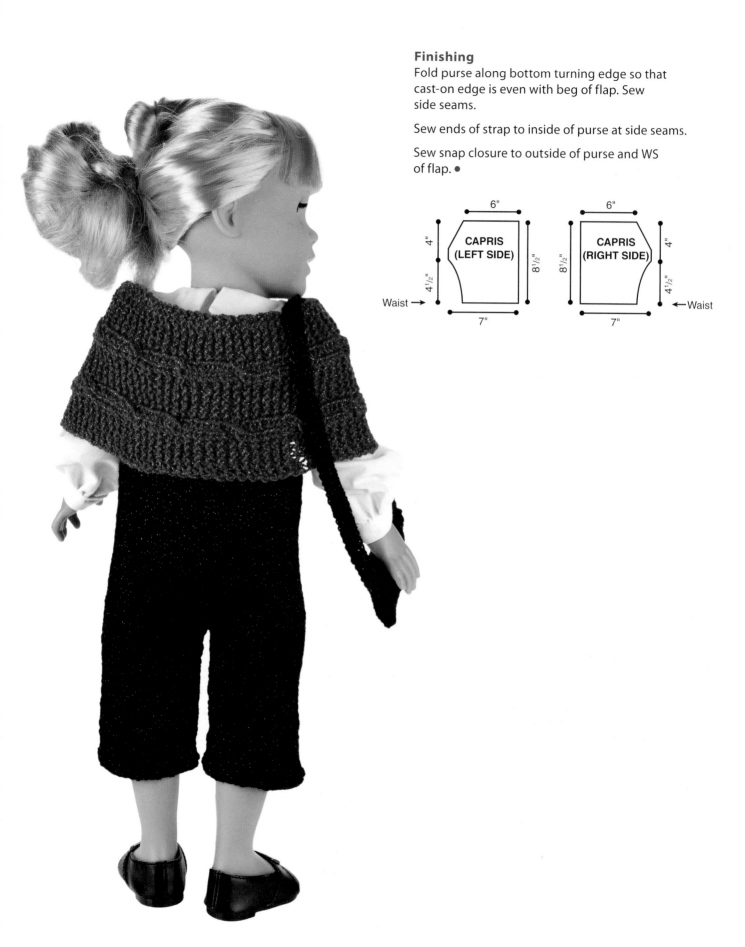

6"

4"

CAPRIS (LEFT SIDE)

8½"

4½"

Waist →

7"

6"

8½"

CAPRIS (RIGHT SIDE)

4"

4½"

← Waist

7"

Beachwear Billie

Size
Fits 18-inch doll

Finished Measurements
Cover-up chest: 14 inches
Cover-up length: 8 inches
Swimsuit chest: 11 inches

Materials
- Lily Sugar'n Cream (worsted weight; 100% cotton; solids: 120 yds/71g; ombrés: 95 yds/56g per ball): 1 ball each hot orange #01628 (MC) and playtime #02741 (CC)
- Size 6 (4mm) needles
- Size 7 (4.5mm) needles, and 1 extra needle for 3-needle bind-off, or size needed to obtain gauge
- Removable stitch markers
- Stitch holders
- 10 (6mm) beads

Gauge
14 sts and 16 rows = 4 inches/10cm in Drop St pat with larger needles.

18 sts and 24 rows = 4 inches/10cm in St st with larger needles.

To save time, take time to check gauge.

Special Abbreviation
Make 1 (M1): Insert LH needle from front to back under horizontal strand between last st worked and next st on RH needle; knit into back of resulting loop.

Pattern Stitch
Drop St (odd number of sts)
Row 1 (RS): K1, *yo, k1; rep from * to end.
Row 2: Knit across, dropping yo's off needle.
Rep Rows 1 and 2 for pat.

Special Technique
3-Needle Bind-Off: With RS tog and needles parallel, using a 3rd needle, knit tog a st from front needle with 1 from back. *Knit tog a st from front and back needles, and slip first st over 2nd to bind off. Rep from * across, and then fasten off last st.

Cover-Up

Back
With larger needles and MC, cast on 25 sts.

Knit 1 WS row.

Work even in Drop St pat until piece measures 8 inches, ending with a WS row.

Cut yarn. Place first and last 6 sts on holders for shoulders; place center 13 sts on holder for hood.

Right Front
With larger needles and MC, cast on 12 sts.

Knit 1 WS row.

Work even in Drop St pat until piece measures 8 inches, ending with a WS row.

Cut yarn. Place first 6 sts on holder for hood; place last 6 sts on holder for shoulder.

Left Front
Work same as for right front, reversing positions of shoulder and hood sts on holder.

Sleeves
Transfer back shoulder sts to 1 larger needle and front shoulder sts to another larger needle.

Using 3rd needle, join shoulders using 3-Needle Bind-Off.

Place a marker on each side of shoulders, 3 inches down.

With RS facing and larger needles, pick up and knit 21 sts between markers.

Beg with Row 2, work in Drop St pat for 2½ inches, ending with a WS row.

Bind off loosely.

Rep for other sleeve.

Hood

Transfer 25 hood sts to larger needle, ready to beg working right front sts.

With RS facing and starting at right front, work across in established Drop St pat, picking up and knitting 3 sts at each shoulder seam—31 sts.

Work even until hood measures 6½ inches, dec 1 st on last row—30 sts.

Transfer 15 sts to a 2nd needle and fold hood in half.

With RS tog, join top hood seam using 3-Needle Bind-Off.

Finishing

Weave in ends. Block piece to finished measurements.

Front Band

With RS facing and larger needles, starting at lower right front, pick up and knit 1 st in each row.

Knit 1 WS row.

Bind off loosely.

Sew side and sleeve seams.

Ankle Bracelet

Thread 10 beads on yarn.

With larger needles and MC, cast on 21 sts.

Row 1 (RS): P1, *slide 1 bead to front of next st, p2; rep from * to end.

Bind off loosely.

Sew ends to form circle.

Swimsuit

Back

With smaller needles and CC, cast on 25 sts.

Knit 2 rows.

Change to larger needles and beg with a purl row, work in St st until piece measures 2 inches.

Inc row (RS): K1, M1, knit to last st, M1, k1—27 sts.

Work 7 rows in St st.

Rep Inc row—29 sts.

Purl 1 row.

Leg openings

Continue in St st; bind off 3 sts at the beg of next 6 rows; bind off 2 sts at the beg of next 2 rows—7 sts.

Work 6 rows even.

Cast on 2 sts at beg of next 4 rows; cast on 3 sts at beg of next 4 rows—27 sts.

Front

Work 10 rows even.

Dec row (RS): K1, ssk, knit to last 3 sts, k2tog, k1—25 sts.

Work 11 rows even.

Eyelet row (RS): K11, yo, k3tog, yo, k11.

Purl 1 row.

Change to smaller needles and knit 2 rows.

Bind off loosely.

Finishing

Leg bands

With smaller needles and RS facing, pick up and knit 26 sts around leg opening.

Knit 1 row.

Bind off loosely.

Rep for other leg opening.

Sew side seams.

Tie

With larger needles and CC, cast on 84 sts.

Knit 1 row.

Bind off loosely.

Thread tie through eyelet holes.

Headband

With larger needles and CC, cast on 52 sts.

Knit 7 rows.

Bind off loosely.

Sew ends tog to form circle. ●

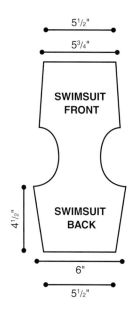

5½"

5¾"

SWIMSUIT FRONT

4½"

SWIMSUIT BACK

6"

5½"

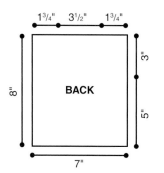

1¾" 3½" 1¾"

3"

8" **BACK** 5"

7"

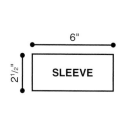

6"

2½" **SLEEVE**

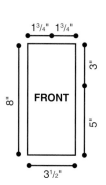

1¾" 1¾"

3"

8" **FRONT** 5"

3½"

Kimono Kimmie

Size
Fits 18-inch doll

Finished Measurements
Chest: 11 inches
Jacket length: 9 inches
Pants length: 8¼ inches

Materials
• Patons Grace (DK weight;
  100% mercerized cotton; 136 yds/
  50g per ball): 2 balls azure #62104
  (MC) and 1 ball spearmint #62902 (CC)
• Size 6 (4mm) needles or size needed to
  obtain gauge
• Removable stitch markers
• 12 inches ⅛-inch-wide elastic

3 LIGHT

Gauge
24 sts and 32 rows = 4 inches/10cm in St st.

To save time, take time to check gauge.

Pattern Stitches
Seed St (even number of sts)
Row 1: *K1, p1; rep from * to end.
Row 2: Knit the purl sts and purl the knit sts.
Rep Row 2 for pat.

Seed St (odd number of sts)
Row 1: K1, *p1, k1; rep from * to end.
Row 2: Knit the purl sts and purl the knit sts.
Rep Row 2 for pat.

Pattern Notes
Jacket is worked in 1 piece from cuff to cuff.

Pants are worked in 2 pieces from waist to cuff.

Jacket

Left Sleeve
With MC, cast on 34 sts.

Work in seed st for 7 rows.

Change to CC; work in St st until piece measures
4 inches, ending with a WS row. Do not bind off.

Body
Using the cable method, cast on 31 sts at beg of
next 2 rows—96 sts.

Work even in St st for 1½ inches, ending with a
WS row.

Shape neck
Row 1 (RS): K48 (back); join 2nd ball of yarn for
front, bind off 7 sts, knit to end—48 back sts,
41 front sts.

Row 2: Working both sides at once with separate
balls of yarn, purl.

Rows 3 and 5: K48; bind off 2 sts, knit to end—
48 back sts and 37 front sts.

Rows 4 and 6: Purl.

Work even until body measures 2½ inches, ending
with a WS row.

Cut CC on front.

Left Front Band
Row 1 (RS): Knit across back; join MC and work front
sts in seed st.

Rows 2–7: Working both sides with separate balls of
yarn, work left front band in seed st and back in St st.

Row 8: Bind off front band sts in pat, and then cut
MC; with MC; cast on 37 sts for right front band; purl
back sts.

Right Front Band
Rows 1–7: Working both sides with separate balls
of yarn, work back in St st and right front band in
seed st. Cut MC.

Rows 8–14: Change to CC for right front; work back
and front in St st.

Shape neck
Rows 1 and 3 (RS): K48; cast on 2 sts at beg of row
of right front, knit across—48 back sts, 41 front sts.

Rows 2 and 4: Purl.

Row 5: K48; cast on 7 sts at beg of front row, knit across—48 sts each side.

Row 6: Cut back strand of CC; using 1 ball CC, purl across.

Work even until front measures 2½ inches from band, ending with a WS row.

Right Sleeve
Bind off 31 sts at beg of next 2 rows—34 sts.

Work in St st until sleeve measures 3¼ inches, ending with a WS row.

Change to MC and work in seed st for 6 rows.

Bind off loosely in pat.

Finishing
Weave in all ends. Block to finished measurements.

Sew side and sleeve seams.

Neckband
With RS facing and MC, pick up and knit 69 sts around neck.

Work in seed st for 6 rows.

Bind off loosely in pat.

Bottom band
With RS facing and MC, pick up and knit 85 sts around bottom edge.

Work in seed st for 6 rows.

Bind off loosely in pat.

Belt
With MC, cast on 6 sts.

Work in seed st for 20 inches.

Bind off loosely.

Pants

Left Side
Beg at waist and using MC, cast on 36 sts.

Work 5 rows in St st.

Hem-turning row (WS): Knit 1 row.

Continue in St st until piece measures 1½ inches from beg, ending with a WS row.

Inc row (RS): Knit to last st, M1, k1—37 sts.

Rep Inc row [every 4 rows] 5 more times—42 sts.

Work even until piece measures 4½ inches, ending with a WS row; place marker at each side.

Work even until piece measures 8½ inches, ending with a WS row.

Work in seed st for 6 rows.

Bind off loosely in pat.

Right Side
Beg at waist and using MC, cast on 36 sts.

Work 5 rows in St st.

Hem-turning row (WS): Knit 1 row.

Continue in St st until piece measures 1½ inches, ending with a WS row.

Inc row (RS): K1, M1, knit to end—37 sts.

Rep Inc row [every 4 rows] 5 more times—42 sts.

Work even until piece measures 4½ inches, ending with a WS row; place marker at each side.

Work even until piece measures 8½ inches, ending with a WS row.

Work in seed st for 6 rows.

Bind off loosely in pat.

Finishing
Weave in all ends. Block pieces to measurements given on schematics.

Sew back seam (inc edge) from waist to the marker. Sew front seam (straight edge) to marker. Sew leg seams.

Overlap ends of elastic and sew tog to make an 11-inch circle. Fold waist hem down along turning ridge covering elastic; sew hem in place. ●

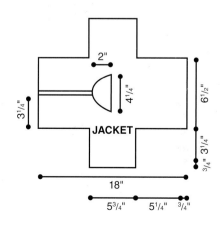

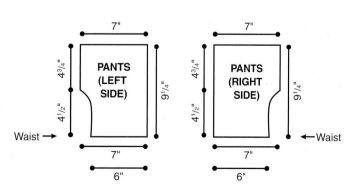

Ballerina Tina

Skill Level
◼◼◻◻ EASY

Size
Fits 18-inch doll

Finished Measurements
Chest: 11 inches
Length: 6½ inches

Materials
- Patons Grace (DK weight; 100% mercerized cotton; 136 yds/50g per ball) 1 ball blush #62416 (MC)
- Lion Brand Yarn Fun Fur (chunky weight; 100% polyester; 64 yds/50g per ball) 1 ball soft pink #101 (CC)
- Size 6 (4mm) needles or size needed to obtain gauge
- Size 10 (6mm) needles

Gauge
24 sts and 32 rows = 4 inches/10cm in St st with smaller needles and MC.

To save time, take time to check gauge.

Dress

Back/Front
Make 2

With larger needles and CC, cast on 68 sts.

Work in garter st for 3 inches.

Next row (WS): K2tog across—34 sts.

Change to smaller needles and MC; knit 4 rows.

Work in St st until piece measures 6 inches, ending with a RS row.

Knit 3 rows.

Bind off loosely.

Strap
Make 2

With smaller needles and MC, cast on 5 sts.

Work in garter st for 4 inches.

Bind off loosely.

Flower
Make 2

With smaller needles and MC, cast on 8 sts.

Row 1 (RS): Knit.

Rows 2, 4 and 6 (WS): Purl.

Row 3: Inc in each st across—16 sts.

Row 5: Inc in each st across—32 sts.

Bind off loosely.

Roll flower into a spiral with purl side to the outside and tack at base.

Finishing
Weave in ends. Block to finished measurements.

Sew side seams. Sew straps to front and back 1 inch in from each side seam.

Sew 1 flower to top center of dress.

Leg Warmers
With smaller needles and MC, cast 39 sts.

Knit 3 rows.

Beg and end with a RS row, work in St st for 3½ inches.

Knit 3 rows.

Bind off loosely.

Sew sides tog to form a tube.

Headband
With smaller needles and MC, cast on 5 sts.

Work in garter st for 12 inches, slightly stretched. Bind off loosely.

Sew cast-on edge to bound-off edge. Sew 1 flower to headband. ●

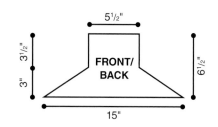

Farmer Frannie

Skill Level
■■□□ EASY

Size
Fits 18-inch doll

Finished Measurements
Chest: 11 inches
Length: 13 inches

Materials
- Caron Simply Soft (worsted weight; 100% acrylic; 157 yds/85g per skein): 1 skein each country blue #2626 (MC) and bone #2604 (CC)
- Size 7 (4.5mm) needles or size needed to obtain gauge
- Removable stitch markers
- Stitch holder
- 2 (½-inch) buttons
- 2 snap closures

Gauge
20 sts and 28 rows = 4 inches/10cm in St st.

To save time, take time to check gauge.

Special Abbreviation
Make 1 (M1): Insert LH needle from front to back under running thread between last st worked and next st on RH needle; knit into back of resulting loop.

Overalls

Left Side
Beg at waist and using MC, cast on 31 sts.

Knit 3 rows.

Beg with a RS row and ending with a WS row, work in St st until piece measures 2 inches.

Inc row (RS): Knit to last st, M1, k1—32 sts.

Rep Inc row [every 4 rows] 3 more times—35 sts.

Work even until piece measures 4½ inches. Place marker on each side of work.

Work even until piece measures 5 inches, ending with a WS row.

Dec row (RS): Knit to last 3 sts, k2tog, k1—34 sts.

Rep Dec row [every 6 rows] 3 more times—31 sts.

Work even until piece measures 10 inches, ending with a RS row.

Work 6 rows of rev St st for cuff.

Bind off loosely.

Right Side
Work as for left side until piece measures 2 inches, ending with a WS row.

Inc row (RS): K1, M1, knit to end—32 sts.

Rep Inc row [every 4 rows] 3 more times—35 sts.

Work even until piece measures 4½ inches. Place marker on each side of work.

Work even until piece measures 5 inches, ending with a WS row.

Dec row (RS): K1, ssk, knit to end—34 sts.

Rep Dec row [every 6 rows] 3 more times—31 sts.

Work even until piece measures 10 inches, ending with a RS row.

Work 6 rows of rev St st for cuff.

Bind off loosely.

Assembly
Sew back seam (inc edge) of left and right sides from waist to marker.

Sew front seam (straight edge) of left and right sides from waist to marker.

With RS facing, sew leg seam to cuff; with WS (St st side) facing, complete cuff seam. Fold up lower edge of pant leg for cuff. Rep for other leg.

Bib
Measure 1½ inches from each side of front center seam and place markers.

With RS facing and MC, pick up and knit 15 sts between markers.

Work in garter st for 2½ inches.

Bind off loosely.

Pocket
With MC, cast on 9 sts.

Work in St st for 8 rows.

Bind off loosely.

Back Straps
Measure 1½ inches from each side of back center seam and place markers.

With RS facing and MC, pick up and knit 16 sts between markers.

Knit 3 rows.

Dec row (RS): K1, ssk, knit to last 3 sts, k2tog, k1—14 sts.

Knit 1 row.

Rep last 2 rows 3 more times—8 sts.

Divide for straps
K4, join 2nd ball of yarn, k4.

Work both straps at once with separate balls of yarn until straps measure 5½ inches.

Bind off loosely.

Finishing
Sew pocket to the center of bib.

Sew snap closures to bib and underneath the straps.

Sew button to the front of straps.

Weave in all ends.

Hat

Crown
Beg at lower edge of crown with CC, cast on 58 sts.

Rows 1–6: Work in St st.

Row 7: K1, [k6, k2tog] 7 times, end k1—51 sts.

Row 8 and all WS rows: Purl.

Row 9: K1, [k5, k2tog] 7 times, end k1—44 sts.

Row 11: K1, [k4, k2tog] 7 times, end k1—37 sts.

Row 13: K1, [k3, k2tog] 7 times, end k1—30 sts.

Row 15: K1, [k2, k2tog] 7 times, end k1—23 sts.

Row 17: K1, [k1, k2tog] 7 times, end k1—16 sts.

Row 19: K1, [k2tog] 7 times, end k1—9 sts.

Cut yarn, leaving 10-inch tail. Place sts on a holder.

Brim
With RS facing and CC, pick up and knit 57 sts along cast-on edge of crown.

Knit 3 rows.

Next row (RS): *K3, M1; rep from * to last 3 sts, k3—75 sts.

Knit 5 rows.

Bind off loosely.

Assembly
With tapestry needle and CC, thread yarn from crown through rem 9 sts, pulling tight. Using same yarn, sew seam.

Weave in all ends. ●

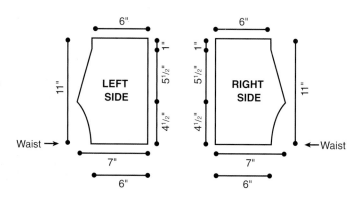

General Information

Abbreviations & Symbols

[ ] work instructions within brackets as many times as directed

( ) work instructions within parentheses in the place directed

** repeat instructions following the asterisks as directed

* repeat instructions following the single asterisk as directed

" inch(es)

approx approximately
beg begin/begins/beginning
CC contrasting color
ch chain stitch
cm centimeter(s)
cn cable needle
dec decrease/decreases/ decreasing
dpn(s) double-point needle(s)
g gram(s)
inc increase/increases/increasing

k knit
k2tog knit 2 stitches together
kwise knitwise
LH left hand
m meter(s)
M1 make one stitch
MC main color
mm millimeter(s)
oz ounce(s)
p purl
pat(s) pattern(s)
p2tog purl 2 stitches together
psso pass slipped stitch over
pwise purlwise
rem remain/remains/remaining
rep(s) repeat(s)
rev St st reverse stockinette stitch
RH right hand
rnd(s) rounds
RS right side
skp slip, knit, pass slipped stitch over—1 stitch decreased

sk2p slip 1, knit 2 together, pass slipped stitch over the knit 2 together—2 stitches decreased
sl slip
sl 1 kwise slip 1 knitwise
sl 1 pwise slip 1 purlwise
sl st slip stitch(es)
ssk slip, slip, knit these 2 stitches together—a decrease
st(s) stitch(es)
St st stockinette stitch
tbl through back loop(s)
tog together
WS wrong side
wyib with yarn in back
wyif with yarn in front
yd(s) yard(s)
yfwd yarn forward
yo (yo's) yarn over(s)

Skill Levels

BEGINNER

Beginner projects for first-time knitters using basic stitches. Minimal shaping.

EASY

Easy projects using basic stitches, repetitive stitch patterns, simple color changes and simple shaping and finishing.

INTERMEDIATE

Intermediate projects with a variety of stitches, mid-level shaping and finishing.

EXPERIENCED

Experienced projects using advanced techniques and stitches, detailed shaping and refined finishing.

Standard Yarn Weight System
Categories of yarn, gauge ranges, and recommended needle sizes

Yarn Weight Symbol & Category Names	**0** LACE	**1** SUPER FINE	**2** FINE	**3** LIGHT	**4** MEDIUM	**5** BULKY	**6** SUPER BULKY
Type of Yarns in Category	Fingering 10-Count Crochet Thread	Sock, Fingering, Baby	Sport, Baby	DK, Light Worsted	Worsted, Afghan, Aran	Chunky, Craft, Rug	Super Chunky, Roving
Knit Gauge Range* in Stockinette Stitch to 4 inches	33–40 sts**	27–32 sts	23–26 sts	21–24 sts	16–20 sts	12–15 sts	6–11 sts
Recommended Needle in Metric Size Range	1.5–2.25mm	2.25–3.25mm	3.25–3.75mm	3.75–4.5mm	4.5–5.5mm	5.5–8mm	8mm and larger
Recommended Needle U.S. Size Range	000 to 1	1 to 3	3 to 5	5 to 7	7 to 9	9 to 11	11 and larger

* GUIDELINES ONLY: The above reflect the most commonly used gauges and needle sizes for specific yarn categories.

** Lace weight yarns are usually knitted on larger needles and hooks to create lacy, openwork patterns. Accordingly, a gauge range is difficult to determine. Always follow the gauge stated in your pattern.

Inches Into Millimeters & Centimeters
All measurements are rounded off slightly.

inches	mm	cm	inches	cm	inches	cm	inches	cm
⅛	3	0.3	5	12.5	21	53.5	38	96.5
¼	6	0.6	5½	14	22	56.0	39	99.0
⅜	10	1.0	6	15.0	23	58.5	40	101.5
½	13	1.3	7	18.0	24	61.0	41	104.0
⅝	15	1.5	8	20.5	25	63.5	42	106.5
¾	20	2.0	9	23.0	26	66.0	43	109.0
⅞	22	2.2	10	25.5	27	68.5	44	112.0
1	25	2.5	11	28.0	28	71.0	45	114.5
1¼	32	3.2	12	30.5	29	73.5	46	117.0
1½	38	3.8	13	33.0	30	76.0	47	119.5
1¾	45	4.5	14	35.5	31	79.0	48	122.0
2	50	5.0	15	38.0	32	81.5	49	124.5
2½	65	6.5	16	40.5	33	84.0	50	127.0
3	75	7.5	17	43.0	34	86.5		
3½	90	9.0	18	46.0	35	89.0		
4	100	10.0	19	48.5	36	91.5		
4½	115	11.5	20	51.0	37	94.0		

Knitting Basics

Cast-On

Leaving an end about an inch long for each stitch to be cast on, make a slip knot on the right needle.

Place the thumb and index finger of your left hand between the yarn ends with the long yarn end over your thumb, and the strand from the skein over your index finger. Close your other fingers over the strands to hold them against your palm. Spread your thumb and index fingers apart and draw the yarn into a "V."

Place the needle in front of the strand around your thumb and bring it underneath this strand. Carry the needle over and under the strand on your index finger.

Draw through loop on thumb.

Drop the loop from your thumb and draw up the strand to form a stitch on the needle.

Repeat until you have cast on the number of stitches indicated in the pattern. Remember to count the beginning slip knot as a stitch.

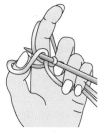

Cable Cast-On

This type of cast-on is used when adding stitches in the middle or at the end of a row.

Make a slip knot on the left needle. Knit a stitch in this knot and place it on the left needle. Insert the right needle between the last two stitches on the left needle. Knit a stitch and place it on the left needle. Repeat for each stitch needed.

Knit (k)

Insert tip of right needle from front to back in next stitch on left needle.

Bring yarn under and over the tip of the right needle.

Pull yarn loop through the stitch with right needle point.

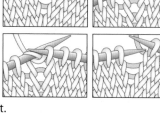

Slide the stitch off the left needle. The new stitch is on the right needle.

Purl (p)

With yarn in front, insert tip of right needle from back to front through next stitch on the left needle.

Bring yarn around the right needle counterclockwise.

With right needle, draw yarn back through the stitch.

Slide the stitch off the left needle. The new stitch is on the right needle.

Bind-Off

Binding off (knit)

Knit first two stitches on left needle. Insert tip of left needle into first stitch worked on right needle and pull it over the second stitch and completely off the needle.

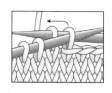

Knit the next stitch and repeat. When one stitch remains on right needle, cut yarn and draw tail through last stitch to fasten off.

Binding off (purl)

Purl first two stitches on left needle. Insert tip of left needle into first stitch worked on right needle and pull it over the second stitch and completely off the needle.

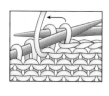

Purl the next stitch and repeat. When one stitch remains on right needle, cut yarn and draw tail through last stitch to fasten off.

Increase (inc)

Two stitches in one stitch

Knit increase (kfb)
Knit the next stitch in the usual manner, but don't remove the stitch from the left needle. Place right needle behind left needle and knit again into the back of the same stitch. Slip original stitch off left needle.

Purl increase (pfb)
Purl the next stitch in the usual manner, but don't remove the stitch from the left needle. Place right needle behind left needle and purl again into the back of the same stitch. Slip original stitch off left needle.

Invisible Increase (M1)
There are several ways to make or increase one stitch.

Make 1 with Left Twist (M1L)
Insert left needle from front to back under the horizontal loop between the last stitch worked and next stitch on left needle.

With right needle, knit into the back of this loop.

To make this increase on the purl side, insert left needle in same manner and purl into the back of the loop.

Make 1 with Right Twist (M1R)
Insert left needle from back to front under the horizontal loop between the last stitch worked and next stitch on left needle.

With right needle, knit into the front of this loop.

To make this increase on the purl side, insert left needle in same manner and purl into the front of the loop.

Make 1 with Backward Loop over the right needle
With your thumb, make a loop over the right needle.

Slip the loop from your thumb onto the needle and pull to tighten.

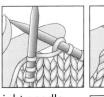

Make 1 in top of stitch below
Insert tip of right needle into the stitch on left needle one row below.

Knit this stitch, then knit the stitch on the left needle.

Decrease (dec)

Knit 2 together (k2tog)
Put tip of right needle through next two stitches on left needle as to knit. Knit these two stitches as one.

Purl 2 together (p2tog)
Put tip of right needle through next two stitches on left needle as to purl. Purl these two stitches as one.

Slip, Slip, Knit (ssk)
Slip next two stitches, one at a time as to knit, from left needle to right needle.

Insert left needle in front of both stitches and knit them together.

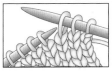
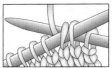

Slip, Slip, Purl (ssp)
Slip next two stitches, one at a time as to knit, from left needle to right needle. Slip these stitches back onto left needle keeping them twisted. Purl these two stitches together through back loops.

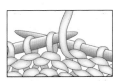

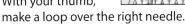
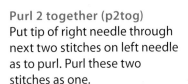

Basic Fringe Instructions

Cut a piece of cardboard half as long as specified in instructions for strands plus ½ inch for trimming allowance. Wind yarn loosely and evenly lengthwise around cardboard. When card is filled, cut yarn across one end. Do this several times, and then begin fringing; you can wind additional strands as you need them.

Single-Knot Fringe

Hold specified number of strands for one knot of fringe together, and then fold in half. Hold afghan with right side facing you. Use crochet hook to draw folded end through space or stitch from right to wrong side (Figures 1 and 2), pull loose ends through folded section (Figure 3) and draw knot up firmly (Figure 4). Space knots as indicated in pattern instructions.

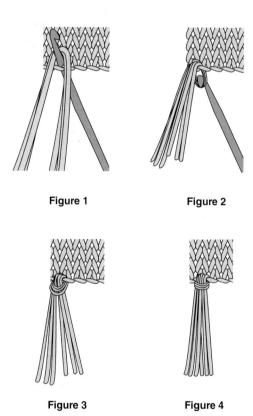

Figure 1	Figure 2

Figure 3	Figure 4

Knitting With Beads

Threading beads onto yarn is the most common way to knit with beads.

Step 1: Before beginning to knit, thread the beads onto your skein of yarn using a bead threader. As you work, unwind a small quantity of yarn, each time sliding the beads toward the ball until needed. Pass the yarn through the loop of the threader and pick up beads with the working end of the needle.

Step 2: Slide the beads over the loop and onto the yarn.

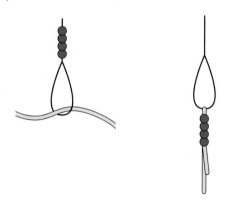

3-Needle Bind-Off

Use this technique for seaming two edges together, such as when joining a seam. Hold the live edge stitches on two separate needles with right sides of the fabric together.

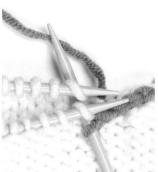

With a third needle, knit together a stitch from the front needle with one from the back.

Repeat, knitting a stitch from the front needle with one from the back needle once more.

Slip the first stitch over the second.

Repeat, knitting a front and back pair of stitches together, then bind one pair off.

Photo Index

4

10

16

21

25

30

34

38

HOUSE of
WHITE
BIRCHES
PUBLISHERS
SINCE 1947

Fun Fashions is published by DRG, 306 East Parr Road, Berne, IN 46711. Printed in USA. Copyright © 2011 DRG. All rights reserved. This publication may not be reproduced in part or in whole without written permission from the publisher.

RETAIL STORES: If you would like to carry this pattern book or any other DRG publications, visit DRGwholesale.com.

Every effort has been made to ensure that the instructions in this pattern book are complete and accurate. We cannot, however, take responsibility for human error, typographical mistakes or variations in individual work. Please visit AnniesCustomerCare.com to check for pattern updates.

ISBN: 978-1-59217-343-3
1 2 3 4 5 6 7 8 9